LOSE WEIGHT THE HEALTHY WAY

CATHY HOPE

To Florence,
who has been
an inspiration
to all of us

TABLE OF CONTENTS

INTRODUCTION

What are your goals?

To look slimmer for your wedding day

To gain a promotion at work

To live a healthier lifestyle

To feel less tired and have more energy

To be able to play with children/grandchildren

To fit into clothes more comfortably

To feel more confident

What ever your goal is make sure you have a plan and stick to it.
Plan when and where you will walk or do your other physical activities. Would it suit you to take your walking exercise before work, during the working day or after work? This exercise programme does involve lifting weights or taking diet pills. All you need to do is *WALK!*

Advantages of Walking

Maintains your weight

Lowers blood pressure

Relieves premenstrual symptoms

Reduces the risk of heart disease

Improves your mood and outlook on life generally

Reduces the risk of diabetes

Increases energy levels

Burns calories

Reduces back pain

Strengthens bones

Reduces stress and helps you to sleep better

Reduces the risk of breast cancer

Improves self esteem

No costly gym membership

Plan your route before you start
Find a route that is flat, even and safe

Equipment
Pedometer
Walking Shoes
Waterproof Top & Hat

How to Use Your Pedometer
Pedometers are a great way to get and stay motivated in your walking routine. And they're really simple to use.

What kind of pedometer should I get?
Like a lot of other gadgets, pedometers come in different sizes, brands, and varieties.

You can get one that is very discreet if you'd like to wear it all day long or at work.

A simple pedometer only records **the number of steps you take** based on your body's movement.

There is a tiny apparatus within your pedometer that moves each time you move your hip in order to take a step.

The pedometer "clicks over" with every step you take.

Wear your pedometer on your belt to record the number of steps you take.

10,000 Steps A Day

The British Heart Foundation (BHF) states 10,000 steps a day (about five miles) can give you a healthy heart and reduce body fat

At the end of this programme you will be able to clock up to at least 12,000 steps a day and maintain a healthy balanced diet

Warm Up to Cool Down Routine

If you're new to walking, start off with slow, short sessions and build your way up gradually.

Warm up for 5 minutes at an easy walking pace before stretching, never stretch cold muscles or you risk tearing them. Incorporate mobility exercises designed to take a muscle and joint through its range of motion.

You will start at the top of your body and work your way down. Start at an easy pace for 5-10 minutes.
Stop and do a stretching and flexibility routine for 5 minutes. Find an upright pole or fence or wall that will support you for leaning into on some stretches.

Then walk for the desired length of time. Walk 30-60 minutes at a pace

Cool down with 5-10 minutes at an easy pace.

End with 5 minutes of gentle stretching and flexibility exercises.

Stretching will make you feel great and assist in injury prevention.

If you are walking for weight loss you should walk a minimum of five days a week, 45 to 60 minutes at a brisk pace.

Walking reduces risks of type-2 diabetes, stroke, cancer, hypertension, and other major diseases.

Walking Technique

Strike the heel first

Swing your arms vigorously as you walk

Remember to breathe in and out

Ensure your back is straight when you walk

Keep your head up, look ahead

Keep shoulders relaxed

Contract abdominal muscles

Stabilise your hips

WARNING

If you ever feel chest pain or pressure, pain in the arms, neck or jaw, lightheadedness or dizziness, palpitations, nausea, blurred vision or faintness, stop exercising and seek help if necessary

1. DAY 1 - 7: START NOW

Day	Exercise Program	Eating Plan
Day 1	5 Min Warm Up 3000 steps 30 minutes Slow Pace Cool down	Breakfast: 1 cup berries with 200g low-fat yogurt *Drink/Snack*: Water & low-fat yoghurt Lunch: Tuna salad: 100g canned tuna, 2 cups mixed salad, 2 slices canned beetroot, 6 olives, with low-fat dressing Dinner: Chicken Mushroom Pasta
Day 2	5 Min Warm Up 3000 steps 30 minutes Slow Pace Cool down	Breakfast: Wholemeal toast topped with Marmite, sliced avocado and grilled bacon *Drink/Snack:* Water & 1 banana Lunch: Mixed Bean Salad with Parma Ham and Rocket Dinner: Lamb with Bean Salad
Day 3	5 Min Warm Up 3000 steps 30 minutes Slow Pace Cool down	Breakfast: Fruit salad; 2 Ryvita topped with 2 slices of cold ham and tablespoon of cottage cheese *Drink/Snack:* Water & chopped baby carrots Lunch: Roast turkey breast sandwich- 2 slices rye bread, roast turkey breast, 2 slices of tomato, shredded lettuce, cranberry jelly Dinner: Vegetable Stew
Day 4	5 Min Warm Up 3000 steps 30 minutes Slow Pace Cool down	Breakfast: Cereal with skimmed milk; glass of orange juice *Drink/Snack:* Water &1 peach Lunch: 1 Chicken and salad wrap: 1 wrap with 60g chicken breast and salad Dinner: Spicy Couscous
Day 5	5 Min Warm Up 3000 steps 30 minutes Slow Pace Cool down	Breakfast: Porridge topped with 1 tbsp of wheat germ and strawberries *Drink/Snack:* Water & 5 strawberries Lunch: Bread roll with rare roast beef, seeded mustard and salad Dinner: Beef with Potatoes
Day 6	5 Min Warm Up 3000 steps 30 minutes Slow Pace Cool down	Breakfast: 2 slices of bacon and 2 tomatoes on wholemeal toast *Drink/Snack:* Water and Melon slices Lunch: 30g tasty cheese on 2 slices bread Dinner: Veal with lemon sage cream
Day 7	**HAVE A REST**	Breakfast: 1 grapefruit and 1 boiled egg *Drink/Snack:* Water & 1 apple Lunch: Crab & grapefruit salad Dinner: Carrot Casserole

2. DAY 8 – 14: MOVE IT!

Day	Exercise Program	Eating Plan
Day 8	5 Min Warm Up 4000 steps 35 minutes Steady Pace Cool down	Breakfast: 1 poached egg with grilled tomato, mushrooms and black pepper *Drink/Snack:* Water & fruit yoghurt Lunch: Cucumber and peach Salad Dinner: Ratatouille
Day 9	5 Min Warm Up 4000 steps 35 minutes Steady Pace Cool down	Breakfast: Porridge topped with Banana *Drink/Snack:* Water & pineapple chunks Lunch: Monk fish and orange salad Dinner: Saffron Vegetable Rice
Day 10	5 Min Warm Up 4000 steps 35 minutes Steady Pace Cool down	Breakfast: Fruit (strawberries, blueberries and banana) & natural bio-yoghurt *Drink/Snack:* Water &1 steamed corn on the cob Lunch : Pita Pockets with avocado and sprouts Dinner: Hot Pot Cannellini Beans
Day 11	5 Min Warm Up 4000 steps 35 minutes Steady Pace Cool down	Breakfast: 10 cherries *Drink/Snack:* Water & chopped baby carrots Lunch: Chicken & Cabbage Salad Dinner: Pasta with fresh tomato sauce
Day 12	5 Min Warm Up 4000 steps 35 minutes Steady Pace Cool down	Breakfast: 2 Weetabix with semi-skimmed milk *Drink/Snack:* Water &1 banana Lunch: Char-grilled Vegetable & Tofu Salad Dinner: Spicy Pumpkin Soup
Day 13	5 Min Warm Up 4000 steps 35 minutes Steady Pace Cool down	Breakfast: Wholemeal bread with Marmite, sliced avocado and grilled bacon *Drink/Snack:* Water and Melon slices Lunch: Prawn, mango and rocket salad Dinner: Chicken & Red Pepper Risotto with Spinach
Day 14	**HAVE A REST**	Breakfast: ½ cup high-fibre cereal with semi- skimmed milk and strawberries *Drink/Snack:* Water &1 apple Lunch: Grilled Salmon with Nicoise Salad Dinner: Black beans and rice

3. DAY 15 – 21 GETTING INTO THE ROUTINE

Day	Exercise Program	Eating Plan
Day 15	5 Min Warm Up 6000 steps 40 minutes Steady Pace Cool down	Breakfast: 1 grapefruit and 1 boiled egg *Drink/Snack*: Water & low-fat yogurt Lunch: Pita Pockets with avocado and sprouts Dinner: Lamb with Bean Salad
Day 16	5 Min Warm Up 6000 steps 40 minutes Steady Pace Cool down	Breakfast: Cereal with skimmed milk; glass of orange juice *Drink/Snack*: Water & 1 peach Lunch: Chicken & Cabbage Salad Dinner: Spicy Pumpkin Soup
Day 17	5 Min Warm Up 6000 steps 40 minutes Steady Pace Cool down	Breakfast: 1 poached egg with grilled tomato, mushrooms and black pepper *Drink/Snack*: Water & 1 banana Lunch: Prawn, mango and rocket salad Dinner: Carrot Casserole
Day 18	5 Min Warm Up 6000 steps 40 minutes Brisk Pace Cool down	Breakfast: 2 Weetabix with semi-skimmed milk *Drink/Snack*: Water & chopped baby carrots Lunch: Tuna salad: 100g canned tuna, 2 cups mixed salad, 2 slices canned beetroot, 6 olives, with low-fat dressing Dinner: Ratatouille
Day 19	5 Min Warm Up 6000 steps 40 minutes Brisk Pace Cool down	Breakfast: Fruity cereal- Nestle Honey Nut Shredded Wheat topped with sliced bananas, grapes, apple and semi-skimmed milk *Drink/Snack*: Water & low-fat yoghurt Lunch: Bread roll with rare roast beef, seeded mustard and salad Dinner: Vegetable Stew
Day 20	5 Min Warm Up 6000 steps 40 minutes Brisk Pace Cool down	Breakfast: 2 slices of bacon and 2 tomatoes on wholemeal toast *Drink/Snack*: Water and 5 strawberries Lunch: Salmon & cucumber sandwich made with 2 slices of wholemeal bread and low-fat butter Dinner: Pasta with fresh tomato sauce
Day 21	**HAVE A REST**	Breakfast: Wholemeal toast topped with Marmite, sliced avocado and grilled bacon *Drink/Snack*: Water and Melon slices Lunch: Wholemeal roll with lean ham, peppery rocket leaves and sliced tomato Dinner: Chicken & Red Pepper Risotto with Spinach

4.   **DAY 22- 28: STICK TO THE PLAN**

Day	Exercise Program	Eating Plan
Day 22	5 Min Warm Up 8000 steps 45 minutes Steady Pace Cool down	Breakfast: 1 grapefruit and 1 boiled egg *Drink/Snack:* Water and 1 apple Lunch: Prawn, mango and rocket salad Dinner: Black beans and rice
Day 23	5 Min Warm Up 8000 steps 45 minutes Steady Pace Cool down	Breakfast: Fruity cereal- Nestle Honey Nut Shredded Wheat topped with sliced bananas, grapes, apple and semi-skimmed milk *Drink/Snack:* Water & fruit yoghurt Lunch: Grilled Salmon with Nicoise Salad Dinner: Beef with Potatoes
Day 24	5 Min Warm Up 8000 steps 45 minutes Steady Pace Cool down	Breakfast: ½ cup high-fibre cereal with semi- skimmed milk and strawberries *Drink/Snack:* Water & pineapple chunks Lunch: Cucumber and peach Salad Dinner: Vegetable Stew
Day 25	5 Min Warm Up 8000 steps 45 minutes Brisk Pace Cool down	Breakfast: 2 Weetabix with semi-skimmed milk *Drink/Snack:* Water &1 steamed corn on the cob Lunch: Chicken & Cabbage Salad Dinner: Carrot Casserole
Day 26	5 Min Warm Up 8000 steps 45 minutes Brisk Pace Cool down	Breakfast: 10 cherries *Drink/Snack:* Water & 1 pear Lunch: Cucumber and peach Salad Dinner: Veal with lemon sage cream
Day 27	5 Min Warm Up 8000 steps 45 minutes Brisk Pace Cool down	Breakfast: Fruity cereal- Nestle Honey Nut Shredded Wheat topped with sliced bananas, grapes, apple and semi-skimmed milk *Drink/Snack:* Water and Melon slices Lunch: Salmon & cucumber sandwich made with 2 slices of wholemeal bread and low-fat butter Dinner: Ratatouille
Day 28	**HAVE A REST**	Breakfast: 2 slices of bacon and 2 tomatoes on wholemeal toast *Drink/Snack:* Water and 1 apple Lunch: Prawn, mango and rocket salad Dinner: Spicy Couscous

5. DAY 29 – 35: YOU CAN DO IT!

Day	Exercise Program	Eating Plan
Day 29	5 Min Warm Up 10,000 steps 50 minutes Brisk Pace Cool down	Breakfast: 1 poached egg with grilled tomato, mushrooms and black pepper *Drink/Snack* : Water & 1 apple Lunch: Wholemeal roll with lean ham, peppery rocket leaves and sliced tomato Dinner: Spicy Pumpkin Soup
Day 30	5 Min Warm Up 10,000 steps 50 minutes Brisk Pace Cool down	Breakfast: 2 Weetabix with semi-skimmed milk and strawberries *Drink/Snack:* Water & low-fat yogurt Lunch: 1 Chicken and salad wrap: 1 wrap with 60g chicken breast and salad Dinner: Saffron Vegetable Rice
Day 31	5 Min Warm Up 10,000 steps 50 minutes Brisk Pace Cool down	Breakfast: Fruity cereal- Nestle Honey Nut Shredded Wheat topped with sliced bananas, grapes, apple and semi-skimmed milk *Drink/Snack:* Water & 5 strawberries Lunch: Tuna salad: 100g canned tuna, 2 cups mixed salad, 2 slices canned beetroot, 6 olives, with low-fat dressing Dinner: Carrot Casserole
Day 32	5 Min Warm Up 10,000 steps 50 minutes Brisk Pace Cool down	Breakfast: 1 poached egg with grilled tomato, mushrooms and black pepper *Drink/Snack:* Water &1 banana Lunch: Pita Pockets with avocado and sprouts Dinner: Chicken & Red Pepper Risotto with Spinach
Day 33	5 Min Warm Up 10,000 steps 50 minutes Brisk Pace Cool down	Breakfast: 3 tbsp sugar-free muesli served with grated apple and semi-skimmed milk *Drink/Snack:* Water & chopped baby carrots Lunch: : Prawn, mango and rocket salad Dinner: Spicy Couscous
Day 34	5 Min Warm Up 10,000 steps 50 minutes Brisk Pace Cool down	Breakfast: 2 Weetabix with semi- skimmed milk topped with banana *Drink/Snack:* Water &1 peach Lunch: Pita Pockets with avocado and sprouts Dinner: Lamb with Bean Salad
Day 35	**HAVE A REST**	Breakfast: Fruity cereal- Nestle Honey Nut Shredded Wheat topped with sliced bananas, grapes, apple and semi-skimmed milk *Drink/Snack:* Water and 5 strawberries Lunch: Salmon & cucumber sandwich made with 2 slices of wholemeal bread and low-fat butter Dinner: Hot Pot Cannellini Beans

6. DAY 36 – 42: STAY ON TOP OF IT

Day	Exercise Program	Eating Plan
Day 36	5 Min Warm Up 12,000 steps 55-60 minutes Brisk Pace Cool down	Breakfast: Fruity cereal- Nestle Honey Nut Shredded Wheat topped with sliced bananas, grapes, apple and semi-skimmed milk *Drink/Snack:* Water &1 pear Lunch: Pita Pockets with avocado and sprouts Dinner: Chicken Mushroom Pasta
Day 37	5 Min Warm Up 12,000 steps 55-60 minutes Brisk Pace Cool down	Breakfast: 2 Weetabix with semi- skimmed milk topped with banana *Drink/Snack:* Water & fruit yoghurt Lunch: Crab & grapefruit salad Dinner: Beef with Potatoes
Day 38	5 Min Warm Up 12,000 steps 55-60 minutes Brisk Pace Cool down	Breakfast: 1 poached egg with grilled tomato, mushrooms and black pepper *Drink/Snack:* Water & pineapple chunks Lunch: Chicken & Cabbage Salad Dinner: Spicy Pumpkin Soup
Day 39	5 Min Warm Up 12,000 steps 55-60 minutes Brisk Pace Cool down	Breakfast: Fruity cereal- Nestle Honey Nut Shredded Wheat topped with sliced bananas, grapes, apple and semi-skimmed milk *Drink/Snack:* Water &1 steamed corn on the cob Lunch: 1 Chicken and salad wrap: 1 wrap with 60g chicken breast and salad Dinner: Ratatouille
Day 40	5 Min Warm Up 12,000 steps 55-60 minutes Brisk Pace Cool down	Breakfast: 1 poached egg with grilled tomato, mushrooms and black pepper *Drink/Snack:* Water & a bowl of fresh fruit salad Lunch: Mixed Bean Salad with Parma Ham and Rocket Dinner: Saffron Vegetable Rice
Day 41	5 Min Warm Up 12,000 steps 55-60 minutes Brisk Pace Cool down	Breakfast: 1 banana, apple or pear, chopped into chunks *Drink/Snack:* Water and melon slices Lunch: Salmon & cucumber sandwich made with 2 slices of wholemeal bread and low-fat butter Dinner: Chicken & Red Pepper Risotto with Spinach
Day 42	**HAVE A REST**	Breakfast: Fruity cereal- Nestle Honey Nut Shredded Wheat topped with sliced bananas, grapes, apple and semi-skimmed milk *Drink/Snack:* Water &1 pear Lunch: Monk fish and orange salad Dinner: Carrot Casserole

7. WELL DONE

Final Tips: *KEEP IT OFF*

Drink eight glasses of water a day
Drink water during and after walking to avoid dehydration

Eat slowly
Sit down and take your time to eat your meal

Don't shop for food when you're hungry
Keep to your shopping list

Spend your time wisely
Bring more balance to your life by doing activities that are more fulfilling. Spend less time watching television,

Do not skip meals & *DO NOT SKIP BREAKFAST*
Avoid the temptation to postpone eating until a more convenient moment. Keep it Regular but reduce intake of food.
Start the day with a healthy breakfast. This will provide your body with fuel so you have the rest of the day to burn those calories

Reward yourself
Not with chocolate or sweets. Get yourself a new CD. Take trip to the zoo or cinema

Time out
When you have a cold or any other minor infection it is wise to reduce the amount of activity you do and rest. Try to factor frequent breaks into your routine.

Checking Your Weight
Weighing yourself too often can have a negative effect on your motivation during your programme. Weigh yourself weekly to get an accurate picture of your body weight

Mix It Up
After the first few weeks, try some strength or resistance training and flexibility exercises in addition to your programme. Supplement your programme with dance, step or martial arts classes.

Reduce Alcohol Intake
Go slow on alcohol because it dehydrates you and it has low nutritional value. It also has a detrimental effect on weight control

Healthier Snacks
Swap your snacks for a healthier option such as a bowl of cereal, a piece of fruit or a handful of nuts. For desserts, mid-morning & mid- afternoon snacks you can have the following; cherries, apple, pear, peach, fruit smoothie, grapes or fruit loaf.

RECIPES

Crab & Grapefruit Salad

1 grapefruit (pink if possible)
300g guacamole
350g crab meat, drained
50g cashew nuts, crushed
2 shallots, finely chopped 2 tsp dill,
3 chopped lemon juice
lime

Peel and segment the grapefruit. Cut into large cubes.
In a bowl, combine the crab, nuts, grapefruit, shallots, dill and lemon juice. Season
to taste. Take 4 glasses and layer alternatively the crab mixture and guacamole,
garnish with a slice of lime and serve. 4 Servings

Mixed Bean Salad with Parma Ham & Rocket

1 x 410g mixed bean salad, drained and rinsed
3 large ripe tomatoes (200g), chopped into bite size chunks
15 black Greek olives (40g), drained from a can in brine
1 shallot, finely chopped and rinsed with cold water
30g fresh Parmesan, finely grated
15g flat-leaf parsley, finely chopped
6 fresh basil leaves, torn into strips
4 slices Parma ham (100g)
1 bag rocket leaves (100g), or rocket/spinach/watercress salad, washed and drained
   2 tbsp (10g) pumpkin seeds

Dressing

2 tbsp extra-virgin olive oil
2 tbsp white wine vinegar
2 tbsp pesto sauce
1 small clove garlic, minced or grated
Salt & Pepper to taste

Mix the beans, tomatoes, olives, chopped shallot, Parmesan and parsley together in a
large bowl. Combine the dressing ingredients in a screw-top jar and shake vigorously.
Pour two-thirds of the dressing over the salad and mix well, leave to stand for 10
minutes before eating so flavours can meld together. Taste and correct salt, pesto,
vinegar, garlic or whatever other flavours you may need.
Just before serving, mix the torn basil leaves into the bean salad. Arrange the Parma
ham on the plate and pile some of the dressed bean salad on the side. Toss the
rocket leaves or the bag of green salad with the pumpkin seeds and the rest of the
dressing, and pile onto the plate. 2 Servings

Monk fish & Orange Salad

850g monkfish
1 fish or vegetable stock cube
1 curly-leaf lettuce
300g strawberries
60g raspberries
90g cherries
75g redcurrants
3 oranges
3 tablespoons olive oil
50g fresh ginger

for the dressing: Juice
of 1 orange
2 tablespoons raspberry vinegar
4 tablespoons nut oil
Salt & pepper

Put the fish in a pan, sprinkle with crumbled stock cube and cover with water. Bring
to the boil, leave to simmer for 10 minutes, then remove from heat and allow to cool
down. Once cool, strain fish from stock

Wash fruit, then dry. Spin salad.
Peel ginger, slice thinly and sauté lightly in a little olive oil.

To make sauce, by combining all ingredients and mixing well.
Arrange leaves and fish on plates decorate with fruit and slices of orange. Sprinkle
with slices of ginger, drizzle with dressing and serve. 6 Servings

Cucumber and Peach Salad

1 cucumber
3 fresh peaches
2 chicken breasts
½ red onion
2 handfuls of rocket
Salt and pepper
1tsp olive oil

Dressing:
2 tsp balsamic vinegar
5 tsp nut oil
Salt and pepper

Mix the dressing ingredients together and set aside.
Cut the chicken into cubes, put the olive oil into a pan, heat and cook the chicken for
10 minutes, turning from time to time. Season and set onto a plate to cool. 4 Servings

Pita Pockets with Avocado and Sprouts

1 whole wheat pita breads, cut in half
1 medium tomatoes, sliced thin
1 cup alfalfa sprouts
1/2 cup cucumber, sliced thin
1 ripe avocados, mashed
1/4 sweet onion, thinly sliced 1
tbsp. lemon juice (or to taste)
sea salt (to taste)
1/4 tsp. cayenne pepper
1/4 tsp. garlic powder
1/4 tsp. onion powder

Mix the onion powder, garlic powder, fruit sugar, sea salt and lemon juice into the mashed avocados. Spread the avocado mixture evenly into the halved pita breads. Evenly layer the vegetables into the halved pita breads. Serve immediately.

Grilled Salmon with Nicoise Salad

3 eggs
125g (4oz) fine green beans, trimmed & halved
2 'little gem' lettuces
1 red onion, thinly sliced
225g (8oz) cherry tomatoes, halved
4 tbsp black olives
4 x 125g salmon steaks
1 lemon, sliced into wedges

Dressing
3 tbsp extra virgin olive oil
1 tbsp lemon juice
½ tbsp Dijon Mustard
1 small clove of garlic, crushed

Place the eggs in a saucepan of cold water. Bring to the boil and cook for 5 minutes. Drain and plunge into cold water, then peel. Steam the green beans for 2 minutes and drain. Tear the lettuce into bite-sized pieces and place in a bowl with the onions, tomatoes, olives and green beans. Heat the grill. Brush the salmon steaks with a little olive oil then cook under the grill for about 2-3 minutes each side. Toss the salad with dressing. Divide into 4 bowls. Place salmon steak on top of each. Slice the eggs into quarters and arrange next to the salmon with the lemon wedges. 4 Servings

Chicken & Cabbage Salad

1 large whole barbecued chicken
4 cups cabbage, finely shredded
4 spring onions, thinly sliced
½ cup finely chopped fresh basil, firmly packed
2 cloves garlic, crushed

2 tbsp sweet chilli sauce
2 tbsp lime juice
2 tbsp fish sauce
2 tbsp water
1 tbsp sugar

Remove skin and bones from the chicken. Cut chicken into small chunks. In a large bowl, combine chicken, cabbage, spring onion and basil. Mix by hand to thoroughly combine.

In a small container with a lid, combine garlic, sweet chilli sauce, lime juice, fish sauce, water and sugar. Tighten lid and shake well, then drizzle dressing over chicken salad. Toss gently to combine and serve. 4 Servings

Char-grilled Vegetable & Tofu Salad

2 red peppers (capsicums), quartered and deseeded
2 courgettes, thinly sliced lengthways
3 baby eggplants (aubergines), thinly sliced lengthways
200g (7oz) whole button mushrooms, stems trimmed, halved
125g (4 1/2 oz) baby corn, halved lengthways
2 1/2 tbsp olive oil
375g (13oz) firm tofu, patted dry with paper towel, cut into 1 cm (1/2 in) thick slices
100g (3 1/2 oz) unsalted macadamias, chopped
1 cup finely shredded basil
2 tbsp white-wine or red-wine vinegar
1 tbsp wholegrain mustard
Salt & freshly ground black pepper

Preheat a barbecue char-grill and flat plate on medium to high. Place the red peppers and courgettes, aubergines, mushrooms and corn in a large bowl. Add 2 tbsp of the oil and toss to coat. Place the red peppers skin side down on the char-grill and cook for about 4 minutes each side, cover with a tea towel and set aside to cool. Place the second courgette and aubergine on the char-grill and cook for 2-3 minutes each side, or just until tender. Transfer to a separate bowl. Place the mushrooms and corn on the flat plate. Cook, turning occasionally, for 3-4 minutes, or until cooked. Transfer to the bowl of vegetables. Brush tofu with 1 tbsp of the remaining oil. Place on the char-grill and cook for 3-4 minutes each side, or until golden. Cut into strips and add to vegetables.
Once the red pepper is cool, peel away the skin and cut the flesh into strips. Add to the other cooked vegetables, along with the macadamias and basil. Toss to combine.
In a separate bowl, whisk together the remaining oil, vinegar and mustard, and season well. Add to the vegetables and toss to combine. Serve. 4 Servings

Prawn, Mango & Rocket Salad

½ mango
4oz/113g cooked tiger prawns
2 large handfuls of fresh rocket leaves
Salt and freshly ground black pepper

Fat-free vinaigrette

Remove the stone from the mango, peel and dice. Place the bowl with the tiger prawns and rocket leaves. Season to taste and toss to combine. Cover and chill until ready to serve. Transfer to a serving bowl before eating and drizzle over the vinaigrette. 1 Serving

RECIPES FOR DINNER

Chicken Mushroom Pasta

6 thin low-fat chicken sausages 2
tbsp vegetable oil
200g button mushrooms, sliced
2 cloves garlic, crushed
425g can-crushed tomatoes, un-drained
Salt and pepper, to taste
1 cup elbow pasta (or your favourite pasta)
150g broccoli florets
½ cup fresh basil leaves, shredded

Add sausages to a saucepan of cold water then place the pan over heat and bring water to the boil. Reduce heat and simmer for 5 minutes, then remove saucepan from heat and drain sausages. Cut sausages diagonally into 3-cm pieces and set aside. Heat oil in a large saucepan; add mushrooms and garlic, and cook, stirring, until mushrooms are soft. Add tomatoes, increase heat and bring to the boil, then reduce and simmer, uncovered for 5 minutes before seasoning with pepper and salt.

Meanwhile, bring a large saucepan of water to the boil. Add pasta and cook uncovered until tender. Add broccoli and cook for 1 minute, then remove saucepan from heat. Drain pasta and broccoli well and then return to pan.
Add tomato mixture, basil and sausages to pasta, and toss gently to combine before serving. 4 Servings

Ratatouille

500g tomatoes
1 onion sliced
1 red pepper
300g courgettes
300g aubergines
2 cloves garlic, crushed
1 bouquet garni (*1 bay leaf, 3 sprigs thyme, 4 large sprigs parsley, 10 cm piece celery stalks with leaves, two 10 cm pieces leek)* Salt & pepper
1 pinch chilli

Prepare vegetables:
Peel and chop tomatoes, pepper, onion, courgette, aubergine and garlic

Sauté onions in a little oil in a saucepan.
Add tomatoes, bouquet garni, garlic, salt and pepper.
Leave to cook gently.
Brown courgettes in a separate pan and add to other vegetables. Repeat
with aubergines.
Add thyme and chilli.
Simmer for at least 30 minutes. 4 Servings

Carrot Casserole

9 carrots, chopped
6 oz. low-fat cheddar cheese, thinly sliced
2 cups milk
1/4 cup dry whole wheat bread crumbs
100g low-fat butter
1/4 cup. flour
1/2 tsp. dry mustard
1 tsp. sea salt
1/4 tsp. celery seeds
1/8 tsp. pepper

In large saucepan, cook carrots for 10 minutes or until tender. In another pan, melt
the butter and stir in flour, salt, seasonings. Add the milk in slowly. Stir until thickened
and bubbly. Remove from heat.

Place 5 cups of carrots in a greased baking dish. Layer half of cheese slices over
carrots. Cover with remaining carrots and place the rest of the cheese slices over top.
Pour sauce over carrots. Top with bread crumbs. Bake in 350 oven for 20-25 min.

Black Beans and Rice

1 lb. black beans
1 medium onion, chopped
1 medium green pepper, chopped
2 cloves garlic, minced
1 bay leaf
1/2 tbsp. oregano
2 tbsp. salt
1 tbsp. ground cumin
2 cups brown rice, cooked
Wash the beans. Bring to boil in water and turn off the heat, and let stand 1 hour.
Pour water off and add fresh water. Add bay leaf and oregano. Bring to boil and then
simmer 2 hours or until beans are tender. Sauté the onion, green pepper, and garlic
in water. Stir into beans with salt and cumin. Add the rice. Simmer 10–15 minutes.
Remove the bay leaf.

Hot Pot Cannellini Beans

2 tbsp extra virgin olive oil
2 garlic cloves, chopped

1 dried red chilli pepper
1 medium onion, chopped
1 tbsp tomato paste
1kg shoulder of lamb, trimmed & cut into chunks
12 baby carrots
12 baby leeks
750ml lamb stock
1 sprig thyme
1 tin cannelloni beans
Freshly ground black pepper & salt
1 tbsp parsley, freshly chopped

Heat the olive oil in a large, lidded dish; add garlic and onion and cook for 2-3
minutes. Stir in chilli pepper. Brown the chunks of lamb in mixture. Remove from the
pan into a plate and then use the residual oil to brown the carrots and leeks

Heat the lamb stock and layer the meat and vegetables in the dish. Add the thyme
and tomato paste and bring to the boil.

Put the lid on the dish place in an oven at medium heat. Allow to cook for about an
hour. Check occasionally and top up with water if hot pot looks dry.

Drain and rinse cannellini beans and stir into hotpot. Season with salt and return the
casserole to the oven for a further 20 minutes. Top with chopped parsley. 4 servings

Lamb with Bean Salad

1 red pepper (capsicum, chopped)
100g mixed lettuce leaves
200g green beans, chopped
1/3 cup light mayonnaise
1 tbsp wholegrain mustard
1 tbsp honey
1 tbsp chopped fresh mint leaves
1 tbsp chopped fresh parsley
1 tbsp lemon juice
Salt and pepper, to taste
Cooking oil spray
8 lamb cutlets

In a large bowl, combine red pepper with lettuce leaves

Bring a medium saucepan of water to the boil. Add beans and cook for 5 minutes,
then remove from heat and drain. Rinse beans under cold water and then add to red
pepper and lettuce leaves

In a bowl, combine mayonnaise, mustard and honey. Mix well and then pour over
salad. Toss well

In a second bowl, combine herbs and lemon juice, then season with salt and pepper.
Spray a heated grill plate with oil. Add lamb cutlets and cook for 5 minutes on each
side until browned and cooked through. Remove from heat and arrange on plates.
Sprinkle herbs over cutlets, and serve with bean salad. 4 Servings

Vegetable Stew

1 tbsp extra virgin olive oil
2 clove garlic, thinly sliced
2 leeks, sliced
2 carrots, sliced
2 small courgettes, sliced
300 ml stock
Thyme & bay leaf
1 tin Puy lentils, drained & rinsed
Freshly ground black pepper
Parsley, finely chopped

Heat the olive oil. Add the garlic, leeks and carrots and stir well to coat with the oil.
Cover and leave to cook on a gentle heat for 5 minutes
Add the courgettes; cover and leave for another 5 minutes then add the stock, thyme
and bay leaf. Allow to simmer until the carrots are tender. Add the lentils and black
pepper and warm through.
Remove the bay leaf and serve in soup bowls with parsley on top. 4 Servings

Spicy Couscous

1 tbsp chopped fresh parsley
1 tbsp chopped fresh mint
½ cup plain low-fat yoghurt
Cooking spray oil
2 medium onions, thinly sliced
1 clove garlic, crushed
2 tbsp, hot curry paste
1 courgette, thinly sliced
2 cups of chicken stock
½ cup frozen peas
2 cups plain couscous
2 tomatoes, chopped
Salt and pepper, to taste

In a bowl, combine herbs and yoghurt, and set aside

Spray a heated non- stick frying pan with oil. Add onions and garlic, and cook, stirring,
for about 5 minutes until onions are soft and translucent. Stir in curry paste and cook
for about 1 minute, then add courgette and cook, stirring, for another 2 minutes. Add
stock and peas, then increase heat and bring to boil. Remove from heat and stir in

couscous, then leave to rest, covered, for 5 minutes. Using a fork, gently stir in tomatoes. Season with salt and pepper
Arrange couscous on serving plates, drizzle yoghurt over and serve. 4 Servings

Saffron Vegetable Rice

Cooking oil spray
1 onion, chopped
1 clove garlic, crushed
½ tbsp saffron powder
2 medium courgettes, thinly sliced
2 carrots, chopped
½ cup frozen corn kennels
1 cup brown rice
2 cups vegetable stock
¼ cup coarsely chopped fresh parsley
Salt and pepper, to taste

Spray a heated non-stick frying pan with oil. Add onion and garlic, and cook, stirring, for about 5 minutes until soft. Add saffron powder, courgettes, carrots, corn and rice, and cook, stirring, for 1 minute
Add stock, then increase heat and bring mixture to the boil. Reduce heat and simmer, covered, for 20 minutes until liquid is absorbed and rice is tender. Stir in parsley, season with salt and pepper and serve. 4 Servings

Spicy Pumpkin Soup

2 tbsp olive oil
1 onion chopped
2 cloves garlic, crushed
2 tbsp ground cumin
½ tbsp ground turmeric
250g sweet potato, peeled and chopped
500g pumpkin, peeled and chopped
3 cups chicken stock
½ cup light coconut cream
2 tbsp chopped chives, to serve
Salt and pepper to taste

Heat oil in a saucepan; add onion, garlic and spices cook, stirring, for about 5 minutes until soft. Add sweet potato, pumpkin and stock. Increase heat and bring to boil, reduce heat and simmer, covered for 20 minutes or until tender. Remove from heat and allow to cool slightly.

Blend soup using an electric mixer, in batches until smooth. Return soup to pan and stir in coconut milk over heat until hot. Season with salt and pepper; Sprinkle with chives. Pour soup into soup bowls and serve

Pasta with Fresh Tomato Sauce

6 medium tomatoes, peeled, seeded and coarsely chopped
½ cup coarsely, chopped fresh basil, loosely packed
2cloves garlic, crushed
2 tbsp extra virgin olive oil
2 tbsp, red wine vinegar
1 red Thai chilli, seeded and finely chopped
375g pasta shells
80g low-fat fetta cheese, crumbled

In a bowl, combine tomato, basil, garlic, half the oil, red wine, vinegar and chilli

Bring saucepan of salted water to the boil. Add pasta and cook, uncovered, for 10 minutes until just tender. Remove from heat and drain. Sprinkle remaining oil over pasta, toss gently to combine

Arrange pasta on serving plates or in pasta bowls, spoon tomato mixture over pasta, sprinkle with cheese and serve. 4 Servings

Beef and Potatoes

½ cup light sour cream
1 tbsp wholegrain mustard
1 cup fresh basil leaves, firmly packed
2 cloves garlic, peeled
1 tbsp lemon juice
Salt and pepper, to taste 100g
baby spinach
1 tbsp pine nuts, toasted
200g bay chat potatoes
500g rump steak, fat trimmed
2 tbsp olive oil

In a bowl of a food processor, combine sour cream, mustard, basil leaves, garlic and lemon juice and season with salt and pepper. Process for 30 minutes, then turn off motor and scrape down the sides. Process for another 30 seconds to obtain a smooth paste
In a salad bowl, combine spinach and pine nuts, and set aside.
Bring a large saucepan of salted water to the boil. Add potatoes and cook, uncovered, for 15 minutes. Remove saucepan from heat and drain potatoes. Cut into thick slices and set aside.
Heat a non-stick frying pan. Add beef and cook for 3 minutes on each side until browned and tender. Transfer beef to a plate, then cover and leave to rest for 5 minutes. Thinly slice beef, add to salad bowl and combine.

Drain the frying pan, then return to heat and add oil. Add potato slices in a single layer. Cook until lightly browned. Add potatoes and salad dressing to salad bowl, toss well and serve. 4 Servings

Veal with lemon sage cream

¼ cup reduced fat mayonnaise
1 tbsp light sour cream
½ clove garlic, crushed
1 tbsp mustard
½ tbsp finely grated lemon rind
1 tbsp lemon juice
2 tbsp finely chopped fresh sage
Salt and pepper to taste
2 tbsp olive oil
500g veal steaks
½ tbsp lemon pepper seasoning

In a small bowl, combine mayonnaise, sour cream, garlic, mustard, lemon rind, lemon juice and sage, and season with salt and pepper. Cover and refrigerate until ready to serve.
Heat oil in a non-stick frying pan, Sprinkle veal with lemon pepper seasoning on both sides and cook for 5 minutes on each side or until browned and tender.
Arrange veal on serving plates. Spread lemon sage cream over veal and serve with 2 cups of salad. 4 Servings

Chicken & Red Pepper Risotto with Spinach

1 tbsp extra virgin oil
1 onion, chopped
1 red pepper, deseeded and dried
300g (10oz) (Risotto Rice)
1.2 litres (2 pints) hot chicken/vegetable stock
125g (4oz) cooked chicken, chopped
125g (4oz) baby spinach leaves
Salt and freshly ground black pepper

Heat the oil in a large saucepan. Add the onion and red pepper and cook over moderate heat for about 5 minutes. Add the rice and continue cooking and stirring for 1-2 minutes, until the rice is translucent and shiny.
Add a ladle of the hot stock to the rice and cook, stirring constantly, over low heat until the liquid has been absorbed. Continue adding the stock to the rice a little at a time and stirring until the liquid has been absorbed, for about 20 minutes. When the rice is almost done, add the chicken and the spinach leaves and stir, mixing evenly. Allow to simmer for 2-3 minutes then adjust the seasoning to taste with salt and pepper and serve hot. 4 Servings

BMI (kg/m²)	19	20	21	22	23	24	25	26	27	28	29	30	35	40
Height (in.)	Weight (lb.)													
58"(4ft 10)	91	96	100	105	110	115	119	124	129	134	138	143	167	191
59"(4ft 11)	94	99	104	109	114	119	124	128	133	138	143	148	173	198
60"(5ft 0)	97	102	107	112	118	123	128	133	138	143	148	153	179	204
61"(5ft 1)	100	106	111	116	122	127	132	137	143	148	153	158	185	211
62"(5ft 2)	104	109	115	120	126	131	136	142	147	153	158	164	191	218
63"(5ft 3)	107	113	118	124	130	135	141	146	152	158	163	169	197	225
64"(5ft 4)	110	116	122	128	134	140	145	151	157	163	169	174	204	232
65"(5ft 5)	114	120	126	132	138	144	150	156	162	168	174	180	210	240
66"(5ft 6)	118	124	130	136	142	148	155	161	167	173	179	186	216	247
67"(5ft 7)	121	127	134	140	146	153	159	166	172	178	185	191	223	255
68"(5ft 8)	125	131	138	144	151	158	164	171	177	184	190	197	230	262
69"(5ft 9)	128	135	142	149	155	162	169	176	182	189	196	203	236	270
70"(5ft 10)	132	139	146	153	160	167	174	181	188	195	202	207	243	278
71"(5ft 11)	136	143	150	157	165	172	179	186	193	200	208	215	250	286
72"(6ft 0)	140	147	154	162	169	177	184	191	199	206	213	221	258	294
73"6ft 1)	144	151	159	166	174	182	189	197	204	212	219	227	265	302
74"(6ft 2)	148	155	163	171	179	186	194	202	210	218	225	233	272	311
75"(6ft 3)	152	160	168	176	184	192	200	208	216	224	232	240	279	319
76"(6ft 4)	156	164	172	180	189	197	205	213	221	230	238	246	287	328

NOTE

Before starting this or any other diet programme, you should consult your doctor. In particular, this should be done with regard to any allergies you may have to the foods, drinks, products or other recommendations contained in this programme. The diet and exercises may not be suitable for everyone. Pregnant women should be especially careful and ensure that their doctor advises that the diet and exercises are suitable for them. If you are taking medication or have any medical condition, you should check with you doctor first.

It is always the responsibility of the individual to assess his or her own fitness capability before participating in any training activity.
While the author has made every effort to ensure that the information contained in this e-book is as accurate as possible, it is advisory only and should not be used as an alternative to seeking specialist help. The author cannot be held responsible for actions that may be taken by a reader as a result of reliance on the information contained in this e-book, which are taken entirely at the reader's own risk.

CONCLUSION
Repeat this programme and make it part of your lifestyle
Enjoy losing weight!

<u>**OTHER RESOURCES**</u>

<u>***Walking Events & Information***</u>

www.thewalkingsite.com provides information about walking

<u>***Walking Organisations/Clubs***</u>

Walking World
Britain's largest online walking guide. Every walk comes with an easy to follow
photographic guide and an Ordnance Survey map www.walkingworld.com

Walking the Way to Health
A joint partnership b/w the BHF and the Countryside Agency, aiming to increase
physical activity and improve the health of the nation.
The site has a walk finder, lists of walking events, details of walking groups
nationwide as well as 'green gyms'
www.whi.org.uk

Racewalk UK

www.racewalkuk.com

Essex Walker
www.essexwalker.org

Park Race Walkers (USA)
www.parkracewalkers.us

<u>***Footwear, clothing & accessories***</u>

Nike www.nike.com

The North Face
www.thenorthface.com/eu

Adidas www.adidas.co.uk
<u>***Gadgets & Accessories***</u>

Pedometers International Ltd
Range of pedometers covers mechanical and electronic models and functions
include number of steps; distance in miles or kilometres; trip time; time of day and
number of calories burned. www.pedometers.co.uk

GearBuyer
GearBuyer features one of the largest collections of sporting goods, ranging from avalanche beepers to whitewater paddles, allowing shoppers to find almost any sporting goods product sold on the internet. We are dedicated to maintaining and expanding a simple-to-use, time and cost-effective environment for the sporting goods consumer.
www.gearbuyer.com

Gaiam Direct
With Gaiam's range of walking fitness tools including pedometers and kits, fitness becomes as easy as a walk in the park!
www.gaiamdirect.co.uk